Also by Daniel-James F. Clarke:

Daylight: A True Story of Childhood Schizophrenia
(with Cynthia Kaufmann-Rose)

FRAGMENTS
My Journey with Schizophrenia

By Daniel-James F. Clarke
Commentary by John F. Clarke, Jr., MD

FRAGMENTS
My Journey with Schizophrenia

Printed in the United States of America

Sunny Day Publishing, LLC
Akron, Ohio 44223
www.sunnydaypublishing.com

ISBN: 978-09903823-6-2

Library of Congress Control Number: 2015954163

For my father, John F. Clarke, Jr., MD.
Without your love, help, and guidance,
this book wouldn't have been possible.

Daniel-James F. Clarke

DISCLAIMER

This writing has the intent of presenting the diary of the daily life of a person with mental illness and professional commentary on each day's entry. It is not intended to treat or advise. Diagnosis and treatment should be placed under the direction of professionals. The writer does not assume any responsibility for the diagnosis or treatment of individual or groups of people with mental illness.

ACKNOWLEDGEMENTS

I would like to dedicate this book to Robert L. Byrnes Ph.D., my psychologist of twenty plus years and Todd M. Ivan MD., my psychiatrist. Together they have saved my life many times. Finally, I would like to thank my caretakers/parents who have grown with me through this tormented life. I view them now as my best and trusted friends.

I would encourage those with schizophrenia and their caretakers not to give up, EVER!

Daniel

FORWARD

This book is a real life experience. Danny, as an Eagle Scout, enjoyed high adventure outings and was actively pursuing weight lifting in hopes of qualifying for the Olympics. It was not until graduate school in engineering and psychology, in his early twenties, that he was hit with the full impact of schizophrenia. This overwhelming condition put an end to his many dreams.

As parents and family we are deeply affected by our loved one's schizophrenia. While professionally, I trained and worked as a board-certified doctor specializing in family medicine, nothing in my background could have prepared me for this. I was not aware of the degree of personal trauma associated with mental illness until it touched our family. We hope that by learning about schizophrenia and mental illness it will help alleviate the hopelessness, shock and depression so universally present with the onset of this illness. Most importantly, for you to remember that where there is hope, there is life.

Danny is a survivor. This book has provided a new purpose for him: one that reaches out to help others suffering from mental illness; a sincerely noble and worthwhile cause.

Dr. John (Daniel's Father)

INTRODUCTION by Dr. John Clarke (Daniel's Father)

This book is in diary form, written and conceived by Danny, who himself has schizophrenia, manic depressive disorder and post traumatic stress disorder. Danny intentionally stopped taking his antipsychotic medication during the time that he wrote the diary. This is not something either our family or his doctors neither encouraged or were aware of, but something Danny did on his own. He did this knowing that the breakthrough of hallucinations and delusions would be more severe and evident. He certainly got the desired effect.

Danny wants to help other people understand what goes on in the mind of a schizophrenic. It is hoped that this book will help people understand schizophrenia by walking in the moccasins of someone with the disease. The reader may be a person with newly diagnosed schizophrenia, his or her family, friends, medical students, medical personnel or just interested people. Our country and the people of the modern world do not understand mental illness. They certainly do not understand schizophrenia. This book aims to change this.

Schizophrenia is a thought disorder characterized by difficulty in understanding and expressing reality. It most commonly presents as auditory hallucinations, paranoid ideation or bizarre delusions. Disorganized thinking and expressive speech are also common hallmarks of schizophrenia. In some subtypes such as catatonic there may be no speech at all.

Because there is an inability to function socially or in an occupation, the person with schizophrenia consequently is poorly understood by society. Accordingly, poverty, homelessness or criminal incarceration are common results of this illness. Sadly, schizophrenia is therefore often equated with worthlessness, homelessness, laziness, being unproductive, criminally aloof or dangerous.

It is my sincere desire that people learn to feel empathy rather than fear upon learning a person has schizophrenia. Human kindness, patience and respect are necessary supports for all illness, but especially for those who contend with mental illness.

The diary format helps the reader walk in the moccasins of the person with schizophrenia and thereby better understand people so afflicted.

Dr. John

October 3 — Diary Entries

10:30 AM

I am Danny. I have schizophrenia with panic disorder. Today I feel quite euphoric with a racy, speedy affect. And my mind is filled with a multitude of thoughts. I was meeting my new neighbor and introduced myself as a writer. I felt ashamed of myself as a handicapped psycho-maniac. I mean I really am plagued by voices telling me, "You're not worthy" and "Kill him, he's just a dumb redneck."

My father was talking to me about energy saving curly-q fluorescent light bulbs. I had a shitload of visual sights of giant pin-wheel candy lollipops. I had to try not to grab them because I was very hungry and wanted to eat one.

1:00 PM

Axil, my Labrador, always seems to know when I am in wonderland and is protectively sticking close to me at this time. He can hear my thoughts. I think he's a psychic dog. Everything seems to be illuminated by an aura that is gold, probably because I have no money to speak of. SSI just barely covers the rent. This writing makes the voices say, "I am a bum and I'll never fully amount to anything at all." Other voices are saying, "Money doesn't buy happiness." I don't know, maybe it does because I sure am frustrated not having any real amount of money.

October 3 — Commentary

Danny's inner thoughts are expressed in the 10:30 am entry. Low self esteem and worthlessness are common feelings harbored by people with schizophrenia, making them appear aloof or shy to the casual observer. The person with schizophrenia may actually be experiencing a hallucination at the time; consequently his or her lack of attention is often wrongly misinterpreted as willful rudeness by the observer.

When you are the observer please try to understand what is actually happening in the mind of the person with schizophrenia that he or she cannot control and that their action doesn't represent willful insult directed to you.

Your reaction is best accomplished by patience and understanding on your part. This controlled reaction formation is the first step in "walking in the schizophrenic's moccasins."

As you learn to control your initial reaction you will soon see the person with schizophrenia open up to you. Perhaps, he or she will even apologize for their momentary inattentiveness, since many with schizophrenia are aware they are having a hallucination yet know that they are powerless to stop it.

Danny's delusion about his dog, Axil, becomes a common theme throughout his diary. Be on the lookout for such delusions in the person with schizophrenia you know.

Try to be understanding. Avoid making impulsive judgments. Learning to be patient, being a good listener and not being impulsive are necessary traits to develop in understanding schizophrenia.

Dr. John

October 4 — Diary Entries

4:00 PM

Mary Elizabeth came over to do her laundry. We were by the second floor catwalk and I heard a deep breathy voice that kept telling me "Jump. You will fly." Another voice that kept saying, "It was time to sing Christmas carols." This latter voice seemed to come from the chipmunk on the tree 10 feet away. Nevertheless, it was a real ordeal to talk to my sister, Mary Elizabeth.

4:30 PM

Axil was telling me to have some coffee since I woke up at 3:30 pm. I am definitely off of my mania that I had yesterday. I am feeling tired and apathetic. This is the affective part of being schizo-affective. I tried to watch the Browns-Bengals football game with my father, but the announcers kept broadcasting my thoughts. This is truly confounding since I can't have control over my thinking. This is why I never watch TV or listen to radios.

5:30 PM

This was happening because I'm on too low a dose of Haldol. If I didn't drop down to 0 mg a day from 30 mg a day I would not have these hallucinations and mood swings.

My moods and feelings are separate from my thoughts. This is a strong indication of schizo-affective disorder.

Another independent variable is my sense of pain. I don't feel any pain. This is different from normal because my L4-5 and L5-S1 discs are ruptured and bulging. I have surgery scheduled and feel no pain.

7:00 PM

Axil just told me that he wants peanut butter on a spoon. I gave it to him which made him very happy. Dad is watching a musical instruction tape for playing the mandolin. At closer examination he's asleep. Axil choked a bit on the peanut butter so I apologized to him. He said that he hates nutty and I should give him creamy. I'm having a hard time thinking over the TV, so I'll stop writing until it's off.

October 4 — Commentary

People with schizophrenic hallucinations complain of constant interruptions of their normal thoughts. Some people with schizophrenia will listen to the voices commands and do what they're told just to get rid of the voices. The person experiencing the hallucinations will often have a disconnected far-off state or appear not to be listening. This is where you can help. Try to be patient. Listen if he or she wants to talk about it. Don't be judgmental. Remember the hallucination is not desired and not turned on or off by a switch. The experience is usually very frightening as can often be seen by sweating and rapid pulse.

Dr. John

October 5 — Diary Entries

9:00 AM

I woke up at 7 am but had to remain in my room for two hours because I was having hypnogoguic hallucinations and confusion. I feel like I'm coming out of the twilight zone. My thoughts are too fractured to describe. I feel as though my brain is plugged into every outlet in the house. My mood is upbeat; however, if it wasn't for my family and doctors I would be hopeless.

My mother has to go to the Social Security office for me. She is my payee. I therefore do not have to go in person, because people see me as normal. This really pisses me off. If someone is missing both legs they are seen as handicapped; however, if someone is mentally ill they are seen as normal until they talk. Therefore, people see me as being lazy, as sapping the government's money. To get along with society, I have to keep my mouth shut around people that do not know me intimately. This stigma of mental illness is horrible because people watch movies like "Psycho" and fear me like some kind of monster. It truly is hell being schizophrenic.

12:00 PM

My dog, Axil, helps me in many ways. He cuddles by me on days when I'm depressed. In addition to that he talks to me when I am in psychotic states of reality. He is a trusted companion, in that; he doesn't talk to anyone else that I know of. Right now I am flooded with way too many thought to write about; however, I will try. Sharing my ideas with you is a very good way of coping. Chipmunks talk a lot more than squirrels. Chipmunks tend to be much happier than any other animal and I can heat them busily chatting to me about getting ready for winter. Axil is saying that he wants more peanut butter, so I told him he'll have to wait until I'm finished writing. People don't realize how fortunate they are whey they have good health. I think that too many people take life for granted and I find myself jealous and angry with them.

3:00 PM

I just got off the phone with my case manager. She said my back operation was approved by Medicaid. This normally takes weeks. She got it approved in 15 minutes because my pain was driving me nuts. Maybe someday I'll meet her to thank her for all of her help over the years. Everything has a foggy aura of light surrounding it. The light is gold. I think this is God. The squirrels in the trees seem to fly from tree to tree.

9:00 PM

I just returned from Wal-Mart to get toiletries. While there I could hear everybody's conversations about me. I was very miserable and couldn't stop sweating. What was a simple shopping trip was soon hell. Now that I'm back home I can cuddle Axil and hope to calm down. Axil says everything will be all right after I take my nighttime medications. I hope he's correct.

11:30 PM

Missing my nighttime dose of Haldol has me close to the threshold of lucidity. Axil, however, says that I'm still a bit nuts. I sincerely hope I can get a good night's sleep for I'm going to bed now.

October 5 — Commentary

Waking up in hell is an experience most of us can only imagine. Here Danny describes it as part of his normal morning. The recurrent thought disturbances in the form of hallucinations and thought fragmentation are present right from awakening. "It is truly hell having schizophrenia" is the emotion experienced by Danny. Try to imagine, if you can, how complete disorientation and inability to formulate any thought process must feel. It is no wonder that many with schizophrenia become withdrawn and apathetic. Some even assume catatonic posturing for days.

Combined treatment helps pull him out of his morning state. This is in the form of medication and family support. Antipsychotic drugs suppress the hallucinations and thought fragmentation. Familiar faces of his family and dog give him strong support that helps stabilize him. I might add that his dog, Axil, plays a very important familiar role by just giving him a friendly tail wag. Axil is friendly to all but mostly towards Danny.

Family support is done with encouraging positive comments. Avoid negative comments or criticism. Try to keep comments and conversation positive. He thrives on this. Family interaction can be negative between other members. A good rule "no arguments at the table" and "keep discussion positive."

Dr. John

October 6 — Diary Entries

1:30 PM

It took me 3 hours to get up and going today. I was plagued by three types of hallucinations that were unusually long in duration. The first type involved my sense of equilibrium. I thought the floor was the wall. This made it impossible to stop holding onto the carpet. Secondly I was experiencing synesthesia. I thought that I could hear what my dog smelled. Synesthesia is the blending or mixing up of the senses. It's very confusing to me. I kept smelling my family calling me to get up. Thirdly were my visual hallucinations of my surroundings. I saw the carpet as grass, the wall was breathing in and out, and the ceiling was vertical.

2:30 PM

Axil and I went down the driveway to get the mail. We were met by my neighbor. Axil reminded me that I had a bad morning and that I must try to control my thoughts. As I talked to my neighbor, I watched his mouth turn into a butterfly and fly away. This forced me to look into his eyes as we talked. Twenty minutes later, I excused myself, turned, and walked back to my house. The driveway turned into a large black snake and scared the hell out of me. I ran around to my back door and made it safely to my house.

5:00 PM

I took a shower and the scrubbing bubble guys were back. Sometimes I think I am cursed because I hallucinate all of the time, even though I am on a shitload of antipsychotic medication.

October 6 — Commentary

Danny is able to explain and identify his hallucinations. These types of hallucinations are important to understand for people who are living with them. Not understanding what is going on with your thoughts is a terrifying experience.

Recurrent hallucinations are like a reoccurring electrical shock. The person being shocked lives in a constant fear not knowing when the shock will come. This is why they appear apathetic.

The person experiencing hallucinations appears aloof and detached. This perceived observation by others adds to their misconception of the total person they are observing. Family members are usually confused by the behavior, however, once they understand the behavior pattern they soon become more empathetic and soon learn to comfort their family member. "Are you having hallucinations?" or "Can I help" do much more to comfort the afflicted person than criticism.

People with schizophrenia live their lives in constant fear. Fear of what others will say. Fear of reoccurring hallucinations. They appear withdrawn and apathetic. This is the same posturing that a caged animal assumes when constantly shocked by an electrical cattle prod.

You can help quell that fear. First realize that the person with schizophrenia is a person who also needs to be treated with love and human dignity. Learn control of your own fears.

Dr. John

October 7 — Diary Entries

11:00 AM

I feel like pure electrical energy. I am one with the universe. I sincerely worry about it going bad.

11:30 AM

This so-called trip has gone awry. I no longer feel so great. I feel like I'm in Hell. I am trying hard to concentrate on writing this down. I think it's time to call my psychiatrist to figure what is making me feel so out of sorts. I am drinking a lot of water because I think it's systemic toxicity of some sort of drug interaction that I'm currently taking. Hallucinations can be frightening and over whelming at times. If it's just hallucinations, I can somewhat deal with it. If bizarre thoughts are combined with hallucinations, that is too much for me to deal with.

1:00 PM

My psychiatrist told me that the Darvocet that I've been taking for pain is the main culprit! This is so common with schizophrenics that psychiatrists no longer prescribe any type of propoxyphene formularies to schizophrenic patients. This fact is so because it has been found to exacerbate severe psychotic disturbances. It interacts with most antipsychotic medications.

1:30 PM

I called my spinal surgeon and informed his secretary of my problem with the Darvocet and asked for Percocet. I also volunteered my psychiatrists phone number so he could verify my request for medicine change since Percocet is commonly abused. In addition, I called my case manager, Melanie, and told her the whole story about the interaction of propoxyphene and psychiatric medications. Melanie was glad because she could relay this information to help others in the same boat as me.

October 7 — Commentary

The type, frequency and repetition of hallucinations vary from patient to patient. Repetitive atypical hallucinations such as Danny's "scrubbing bubbles" can be bothersome. Danny has been so frightened by these that he is afraid to take a shower.

The most common hallucinations are auditory but hallucinations can be of any type. As Danny had mentioned in his 10-6 entry synesthesia, or the mixing of senses, is confusing and frightening because of losing contact with reality.

Delusional atypical hallucinations are difficult to deal with for the same reason. His believing that Axil can talk to him tests his grasp of reality but it is excused because it is delusional and part of his illness.

It is now known that there are many drugs, recreational or prescribed, that can interfere with psychotic medications. These drugs can precipitate psychotic episodes and should not be taken unless prescribed by a physician.

Hallucinations that are sensual certainly do not create pleasure for Danny. He will tell you he feels like he is in Hell. His worse hallucinations are the complex psychotic ones. These cause fear and withdrawal. The fact that he can talk about these makes them tolerable.

Dr. John

October 8 — Diary Entries

2:00 PM

Now that I have not taken any Darvocet for 48 hours I am not having the mood problems as much. I, however, haven't slept since yesterday because of pain. I seem to dream while I'm awake. Axil keeps talking about wanting cuddling because he hasn't been held by me a lot for the last week. I have been holding him as a means of security when my hallucinations have gotten too severe. He, of course, loves it. I truly think that all people with psychosis should have a dog in lieu of a security blanket.

7:00 PM

Pain in my back is driving a lot of hallucinations. Two hours ago I thought I was in the middle of an ocean on a floating blanket with sharks swimming around me. I pinched myself to see if this was real and I felt it. Usually my hallucinations are so real that I often wonder what reality is. Sometimes I have to ask my parents if someone or something is real or not. I believe that I can see God and He talks to me. He is different than voices that I hear that are not real. God never tells me to harm myself or others. God tells me to refrain from some actions that are wrong while I am in a mania and encourages me to be a humble, loving person.

The typical people who talk in my head, according to others, talk in threats e.g. "Don't step on the crack." "You will win the lottery if...", or "this person is going to Hell.", and "Hurt this person or you'll..." I don't know whether these voices are real or not when I'm hearing them. I often will ask someone near me if they hear something. I never say "what" I heard because people will really think I'm crazy.

10:00 PM

Dinner was most amazing, perogies and sausage. The sausage looked like penises so I avoided them, especially after they pissed on the plate. I could barely eat the perogies because they kept saying over and over, "Eat me and die." Oh well, I just watched the honey container which was shaped like a honey bear moon walk on the table just like Michael Jackson. I need to lose weight anyways.

10:30 PM

Axil and I cuddled on the floor and bitched about the lousy weather outside. Axil and I are dependent on each other. I take care of him and he calms me when I am in a manic state, cheers me when I'm depressed, and cuddles me when I'm hallucinating.

Tonight he will cuddle me. I keep wondering when the damn TV will stop broadcasting my thoughts. The news is the worst tonight, so Axil and I are watching wrestling. Now that is some real entertainment. Axil agrees. Oh well, I'm going to have a cigarette and watch Axil laugh at the professional wrestlers.

October 8 — Commentary

Danny has a lot of pain but refuses to take pain medication because of a fear of exacerbating his schizophrenia. He feels the mental pain caused by the schizophrenia is worse than his back pain. He has rejected chiropractic treatment, largely because of me. He is scheduled for spinal fusion surgery before the end of the year.

Danny has strong family support in place. This is important in the treatment plan for long-term mental illness. Family understanding and support is necessary in helping people with schizophrenia. This support helps lenghten their lives. A lack of support leads to the shorter average life span of people with shcizophrenia. As would be suspected, the incidence of suicide is much higher than the general population.

Dr. John

October 9 — Diary Entries

2:30 PM (at my bother's house)

My mom took me over to my brother's house. I like going there because he accepts me as a person. This is paramount to me, for most people see me as a freak and judge me as a person that can't snap out of it. My brother's wife is always an uplifting person to be with as well. I feel very at home here.

3:30 PM (at Chrysler service place)

There's a TV in the background. I just know the people in this place are trying to distract me, so they can talk about me. I hate this. I want to smash the TV in this car dealership. I saw a Dodge Challenger that was lonely in the showroom. It needs me to drive it. I like to drive fast. Sometimes I like to play chicken. Unfortunately no one lets me drive their car.

4:00 PM (back home)

Axil really missed me while I was with my mom getting her car fixed. He hopped up and down on his front paws greeting me... I love him so much and I can't stop wondering what life would be like when he dies. He's currently 11 years old and in poor health. I often get fixated about this and really get distracted from daily things.

5:00 PM

Colors around me have taken on a neon glow to them. Everything is one and one is everything. I was looking at a tree that just turned into a flock of birds and flew away. The fall colors are absolutely beautiful. I can feel the flow of life energy amped up with electricity flowing through my veins. I wonder what color my blood would be if I cut myself. I bit my arm to see the darkness flow through my shirt. My mom told me not to harm myself but it was too late. I was already leaking. It's really funny when I'm hallucinating. It's just really, really funny. I am for some reason tripping out of my mind. It's time to take 10 mgm of Haldol.

October 9 — Commentary

The entries of this day may leave the reader confused. This is due to the lack of coherence and fragmentation. The thoughts are a blend of psychotic hallucinations and delusion. As you read this diary you can see the torment going on in Danny's thoughts. You may wonder how one can hang onto reality. You can see why without medical intervention suicide is more common. The recurrent themes of paranoia and hallucination are again present.

Towards the end of the day there is a spontaneous return to realizing that he is losing control and needs medication that he was instructed to take by his psychiatrist.

Danny's love of his dog and family help him to hang onto reality. Haldol, haloperidol, is a prescription antipsychotic medication that acts by suppressing the dopamine activity in the mesolimbic pathway in the brain and thereby controlling the abnormal thoughts.

Dr. John

October 10 — Diary Entries

1:00 PM

I'm feeling depressed and apathetic today. All I want to do now is lay down and let the rest of the world pass on by. I woke up and it has taken me four hours to start this diary entry. Thoughts of worthlessness pervade my mind. I just do not feel that great. This is a whole brain and body thing. To me, when I feel up or down mentally, my body feels up or down. I take Lamictal to stabilize my mood; however, I still have mood swings cycling up and down... I love mania and hate depression. On the positive side, I know that this depression is not going to be permanent. That is why I haven't committed suicide. Sure I occasionally get suicidal, but that's when I go to the psychiatric ward in the hospital. If I have any lifelong motto, it is: "Never Surrender"! I plan on getting this tattooed on my left shoulder. I've stayed alive several times by repeating this motto over and over again and again. In addition, I have a great deal of faith in God. This is paramount. Faith keeps me going many times in my life.

October 10 — Commentary

Apathy and depression are again the dominant themes on this day. Danny lets us in on a little secret here in that he knows the mania will follow the depression and he clearly states that he "loves mania" and "hates depression". The mania here and depression are part of his mental illness and usually present together in no particular sequence.

Dr. John

October 12 — Diary Entries

12:00 PM

I could not sleep last night because I am manic again. I feel euphoric and am having a lot of hallucinations. On the other hand I am afraid to take a shower because of the scrubbing bubble guys. They scare the wits out of me. Mania is like being on cocaine plus methamphetamines with the absence of rapid heartbeat.

1:00 PM

I still lack the courage to take a shower; however, I will have to face my fears sometime today. The main reason most schizophrenics appear to be unkempt and dirty is when they have to close their eyes while taking a shower. In addition, the noise of the shower elicits audible hallucinations. I almost always hear voices calling my name while in the shower. This is quite unnerving to me. I also see rats climbing up and down my legs. Even though I don't get bitten, this is terrifying me.

1:30 PM

The leprechauns are outside my door again. These things piss me off to no end. I can not go outside until they return to their hollow tree. This sucks. I hate being trapped inside my house. The leprechauns are about 3 feet tall, look like dwarfs, have red hair, are thin, wear green, and have green Irish hats; you know the ones with the black belts. Instead of having human teeth, they have what looks like canine teeth all around their black-tipped mouths. They keep saying, "Give me my gold." Only my dog, Axil, is not afraid of them. He acts like he doesn't see them.

2:30 PM

My scalp has bugs and maggots crawling in it. I think I'm going to have to take a shower to wash them out. When this type of neuro-sensory hallucination happens too often I usually shave all the hair off of my head, This really pisses my mom off, because she says I look scary. Being 6'2" and weighing over 250 pounds I can appreciate her opinion. Oh well. I'm off to the shower.

4:00 PM

I took my shower and heard people calling my name over and over. I washed as quick as I could. I think that I was too quick for now my skin is all itchy from soap left on it.

6:30 PM

My dad's dog, Molly, spoke to me for the first time. She must be learning to speak for all she said was "Hey Danny." This is just the way Axil started talking. People say that dogs do not talk. Maybe people do not take the time to sit down and listen. Axil has a vocabulary of approximately 84 words.

9:00 PM

I'm feeling so much energy from the manic state that there is no difference between what is in my head or outside. I am hearing the voices of 4 people locked in argument over what I am to do next. I think it is time for another 10 mgm of Haldol. It should get better in 20 minutes or so, but I'm not holding my breath.

October 12 — Commentary

This day's entry is especially good because he has several entries that give us a good look into the workings of his mind. You should be able to see the recurrent hallucinations and delusions with which you have become familiar thus far. Danny has more comments on this day, which reflects his manic state.

A new delusion first appears here which has also been bothersome to Danny. This one usually results in his shaving his head. A delusion may appear to be innocent and logical but on closer examination it is a delusion, it usually answers the question "why?"

The persistent delusion of being able to talk to a dog is expanded here to include Molly, a black Labrador, our other family pet. It may be difficult to tell when a recurrent hallucination becomes a delusion such as his recurrent "scrubbing bubbles" or "leprechauns." Danny experiences both as a recurrent theme. Both cause fear. Both are believed by Danny and are a part of his everyday experiences and therefore fall more into the category of delusion.

Dr. John

October 13 — Diary Entries

2:00 PM

I cannot believe that I slept 15 hours. It must have been the extra 10 mgm of Haldol I took yesterday. I feel as though I am looking at the world through someone else's eyes.

3:00 PM

I am still having this "out of body" feeling. I called Dr. Ivan, He said that this would pass, but in the meantime, he said to avoid looking into mirrors. I don't know what that meant but I am not going to try and find out. The Patriot Act was renewed. This means that all calls and E-mails could be monitored by the NSA. This makes me even more paranoid than usual. Paranoia sucks. I am so sped up that I am hearing Axil sing with two or more voices at the same time. I think that he sounds possessed. Today is definitely a day of mental torture and pain. I would gladly trade just about anything to be a normal person, but I will never surrender.

4:30 PM

I just got off of the phone with the cable company. The woman
in the technical department obviously did not know her ass
form a hole in the ground. I am angry right now.

9:30 PM

I still feel racy. I'm glad to be seeing my psychiatrist tomorrow
afternoon. Maybe he'll be able to help with my mood swings.
Hallucinations have been a part of my whole life. I am able to
deal with them more than the bi-polar mood cycling.

October 13 — Commentary

The events of this day are not normal but this does represent a typical day for Danny. It is tough enough for him to get through a day of hallucinations and then, in addition, have to deal with a day of mood swings from bi-polar disorder. He has become hardened to the hallucinations because they are so numerous. He manages to get through them.

The recurrent delusion and hearing Axil sing is actually a psychotic hallucination. This reflects the complexity of Danny's illness. The importance of this entire day demonstrates Danny's strength and determination to deal with his illness.

Danny is a survivor. Others might succumb to the voices. Danny has developed coping mechanisms through the help of his doctors over a long period of time.

Dr. John

October 14 — Diary Entries

3:00 PM

Today I get to see Dr. Ivan, my psychiatrist. I am anxiously waiting for my mom to pick me up. I hope that I can pick up a bag of tobacco at the cigarette outlet by the doctor's office. Personally I have never heard of a schizophrenic who doesn't smoke. There's something about tobacco that hits the cingulated gyrus in the brain. The cingulated gyrus is the pleasure center, Nicotine affects the schizophrenic brain like cocaine.

5:00 PM

Dr. Ivan said that I need to increase Haldol from 20 mgm a day to 30 mgm a day. He also added lithium carbonate, 300 mgm twice daily. I sincerely hope that these changes will decrease my hallucinations and level out my bipolar cycles. I have taken lithium in the past and have had great success. The Haldol will not stop my hallucinations, but tone them down to a more functional state of being.

9:00 PM

I know that I'll probably sleep in tomorrow because of lithium.

This happens just about every time I go on Lithium.

October 14 — Commentary

After over 20 years of having his mental illness Danny has learned several important lessons that need to be emphasized. These can be summarized here as compliance, importance of establishing a professional relationship with his doctor and knowledge of his medication.

First, he has learned to be truthful with his doctors and knows he must keep all appointments on time or call in for rescheduling in plenty of time if he can't make an appointment.

Secondly, he has learned to be respectful of their time including after hours calls. He has learned to be honest and give full disclosure when and where needed. Lying is simply not tolerated. I suppose he has been coached in these habits by me.

Thirdly, he has learned about his medications including desired effects, side effects and any other new effects not expected. He knows about drug interaction and reports everything to his doctor.

Dr. John

October 15 — Diary Entries

5:00 PM

I just woke up after yesterday's going to bed at 11:00pm. The lithium really kicked my ass. The tiredness will probably fade as time goes by. Axil woke me up with his muzzle saying, "Get up it's already night-time." Axil gets plenty of dog food for dinner, for he woke me up at 9:00 am this morning, so I could take my morning dose. Then I quickly went back to sleep.

6:00 PM

We are going over to my brother Joe's soon. This makes me happy, for I always leave with an uplifted state of being. Axil says he wants to go also, but he would have to stay with the other dogs in one room in the basement. I tried to explain this to him. He wants to go anyways. He would not change his mind and pouted with his head down and away from me.... I feel very sad about this issue.

11:00 PM

I was and am currently plagued by voices. Some are telling me that I am Jesus and others are telling me to kill anyone who approaches me. My anxiety level has sky-rocketed.

11:00 PM

This entry is most difficult since the voices are shouting at me and telling me that I'll never amount to much. And if I don't get a lottery ticket tomorrow I'll surely die or worse I won't get over this anxiety attack.

I'm starting to pull out of this attack. I feel as though every nerve in my body is about to explode. At least I can breathe more freely than before. My heart is slowly starting to relax. The voices are telling me I am doomed. Well, I say nay. My outlook is better because I have successfully pulled out of my harsh state of anxiety.

October 15 — Commentary

Danny's day as can be seen from his diary soon falls into a very characteristic hum-drum pattern of daily hallucinations and persistent delusions. The reader may think of this as a boring existence and become bored with the reading. Danny has come along way from his initial onset over twenty years ago. He may never get any better than he is now. He knows and accepts this. He didn't ask for this, but it happened. Our medical management is directed at control, not cure.

Dr. John

October 16 — Diary Entries

12:00 PM

I did not fall asleep until 4:00 am, because of the voices. I could hear whispering and talking between two teenage girls. It was not what they were saying about me that bothered me; it was, however, the constant giggling and laughing that drove me up the wall. After a long wait I finally slept. I awakened a few minutes ago, refreshed and ready to take on the world.

1:00 PM

There's a crow outside speaking "nevermore" repeatedly. Gee, I wonder where that came from. The trees are breathing slowly as if they were trying to meditate. Axil is telling me that I should try to meditate with the trees. First it is too cold and wet outside. Secondly I am not a tree and don't speak their language.

3:00 PM

Axil woke me up after a brief nap saying, "Get up daddy." He always wakes me up when he has to pee. It could be in the middle of the night. If he has to pee he will wake me up. The air outside looked like cold root beer. If I wasn't cold, Axil and I would be sitting on the porch sipping lemonade. Sometimes I wonder if I am possessed by some dark entity. All of this torment and suffering tests my entire wish for living.

3:00 PM

Sometimes I pray that I would have a heart attack and die! I really mean it. If it wasn't for my family I would have checked out 20 years ago, even this very moment. My family is the only thing keeping me alive.

October 16 — Commentary

Daily life for Danny is filled with bizarre hallucinations. His recurrent delusion resurfaces. Every day he has to battle getting through his hallucinations. The delusions are easier because he accepts them. He can tell you about the hallucinations although he will sometimes tell you he thinks it was a hallucination but is not sure. This is his way of asking my help in analyzing the experience. This also strengthens his coping mechanisms.

Family support is one of the mainstays of treatment. The family can be extended here to include extended family and close friends. Often the friend is someone else with a similar mental illness. Then the support can be mutual.

The supporting person does not have to be a professional person. Sometimes, the support can come from a pet. Sometimes a carefully chosen pet dog can do a world of good for a person with schizophrenia.

Dr. John

October 17 — Diary Entries

12:00 PM

Some police cars pulled up to our house. I did not know why, so I went to my room... It turns out that they were here to talk to my mom about harassing letters my family was getting from tax attorney's offices. I had to close my eyes until 5 seconds had passed to see if they were real. Well they were real.

2:00 PM

At this moment, I am watching the road turn into a river and foliage turn into a tropical paradise. This, and the temperature climate, makes me believe in heaven. Now it is gone and I'm cold. Life makes no sense to me. We are put on this earth (hell) and told that life is a gift. We are, at least some of us, afraid to die. I think that is total bullshit. We are put on this earth to suffer. And those who suffer the most and the longest, win a prize. Why can't those who suffer just go to heaven and skip the pain and agony that is called life.

4:00 PM

Axil wanted to go outside, so I obliged. He showed me that it was a sunny day.

Axil is my best friend in the whole world. Dog he may be but he communicates like a human with E.S.P. I know his thoughts and he knows mine. When I'm suffering a bit too much, he takes me to a change of scenery, so I may get a different mindset. I am feeling better now.

5:00 PM

My parents got home and brought pork from the pig roast they were at. The pork was great, for it was very tender. I think that I'm going to take a nap with Axil.

9:00 PM

I am rested, but I am not exactly sure. I still feel very tired. I get tired like this when I am starting out on Lithium, in addition to 7 other prescriptions. Axil will be happy if he gets a hard-boiled egg. He is happy because he just got one from mom... I am puzzled about "normal" people, all they do is complain about this or that and never realize just how bad they could have it. They could be among the abnormal like me.

October 17 — Commentary

The entries on this day are similar to other earlier days. There are some characteristic traits of schizophrenia seen on careful examination. The entries are choppy, fragmented and fail to flow in a cohesive manner. They are always egocentric reflecting his narcissistic world of schizophrenia. The hallucinations are easy to recognize by now as are the delusions.

Danny's concern over the meaning of life shows that he has the mental capacity to raise deeper philosophic concepts that many people with schizophrenia simply cannot. No two people with schizophrenia are exactly alike. Many have special skills. They may, for example, be skilled in expressive media such as creative painting, music, or writing or in science skills such as math, astronomy or physics. They are usually of a higher IQ than average.

Dr. John

October 18 — Diary Entries

9:00 AM

I am smelling and tasting all of the beautiful colors of fall. This synesthesia occurs to me at least two times per week. I am actually starting to enjoy it, especially when I can see sound.

12:00 PM

The last 2 hours seemed to have passed by in 20 minutes. Today my perception of time is quite a bit off. I did not sleep. Rather I've been hearing voices telling me to cuddle Axil, for he's ill and might die soon. This was more discerning. I love Axil and would miss him greatly should anything happen to him. Axil helps me get through tough times, and I love to hold him, talk with him, and cry with him.

5:30 PM

I've been staring off quite a bit. Lately, I doubt when I am in a lot of pain. Mental pain is 1000 times greater than physical pain. I went through my first back operation awake. I screamed a lot but this doesn't compare to a psychotic panic attack. Granted, panic attacks are bad, but when in wonderland, you pray for death.

October 18 — Commentary

I want to direct the reader to later entry on this day. Here you can almost feel the pain as you stand in Danny's moccasins. Mental pain is severe to those who experience it.

Try to imagine yourself or your loved one waking up every day tormented by voices, depression, run-away mania, or panic attacks. Fear, apathy, withdrawal, paranoia, or panic becomes your dominant feeling. Yes, it's painful.

Dr. John

October 19 — Diary Entries

11:30 AM

My sister, Mary, popped over to do laundry. She is the head chef at a major restaurant. We always have a lot of cooking questions for her.

7:00 PM

Went to see the surgeon today and booked a double fusion for my back. Like I said, physical pain is nothing compared to mental pain. However, when you (I) have both, it's unbearable. Right now I ignore the back pain and suffer the mental anguish. Axil is telling me to cuddle him on the floor, thereby lessening the back pain, while focusing on a stop-block coping strategy.

8:00 PM

Well the coping strategy only seems to work while practicing. Thought stopping can not work while holding a conversation. I am now not using it and the crazy thoughts are back. The voices are now telling me I will die while under anesthesia. Sure this is possible, but it's a small possibility.

9:00 PM

Malevolent voices are wrecking my ability to concentrate. Three voices are telling me to turn the ancillary lights on, while 12 voices are telling me that I must give in to Satan's will. I have not been watching any horror series lately. However, the voices still keep pestering me. I think this part of insanity is the worst.

October 19 — Commentary

The day starts out normal with some normal thoughts that progress to abnormal by the last entry. Normal thoughts are present on awakening but only if he has taken his medication on schedule. When Danny sleeps in or takes his medication late his thought process degenerates. This is very infrequent because he is very responsible about taking his medication on time.

Significant normal life stresses can also affect his thought processes. Normal family stresses can also bring on thought disorder. Coping strategy will not work in the presence of increased life stress, which increases the dopamine level. It is therefore important to try to avoid normal life stress.

Danny recognizes his hallucinations as such and seems to have developed a tolerance to live with these. He does not, however, do well with stress. Careful avoidance of stress by his family helps to make his life more livable.

Dr. John

October 20 — Diary Entries

12:00 PM

My thoughts are too many to count. I'm in a mediocre mood, but am overwhelmed at this time to write very much... My mind is so full of bizarre thoughts that I must meditate at this time.

2:30 PM

I am too troubled to write at this time.

October 20 — Commentary

Stress is causing an increase in Danny's symptoms to the degree that he cannot function or write on this day.

Dr. John

October 21 — Diary Entries

6:00 PM

Today has been a rough day mentally. I was experiencing synesthesia all say. This made it impossible to write. Right now I am getting some visual hallucinations and some voices. The voices are telling me to tell my mother and father that "I love them", because, I'll probably die in surgery on the 27th. They are also saying, "Turn off the lights". All of these statements end with "or something horrible will happen". The leaves on the trees are changing colors like huge misshapen Christmas trees. The cars passing by are tracking. This means as they pass their images are going in several steps at once, and then the steps catch up with the final stages (the cars).

7:30 PM

It's dark outside. Throughout my whole life I've been afraid of the dark. A night-light does not help. At least one lamp must be turned on. I've hallucinated for as long as I can remember. The dark exacerbates visual hallucinations. I was just in my room and my lamp went out. I saw and heard the boogey man. This was disconcerting, horrifying at the least.

9:00 PM

I am very paranoid right now, This is very frightening for me. I just took my medications and I hope they will "kick in" soon. Maybe this is combined with an anxiety attack... All I know is that I'm afraid that I might shit myself out of fear. Everything is glowing orange. I'm afraid someone's going to kill me. I do not know who or how. Mom and Dad said that my subconscious thoughts are surfacing. I'm projecting fear of death in my surgery onto paranoia.

October 21 — Commentary

Danny does not do well with stress. Here it is obvious that he's been thinking about his coming surgery. The content of the hallucination is rather self explanatory. What he does not know is that his concern is even greater because a family member suffered a stroke during surgery. This is obviously why he is so concerned.

Danny is very typical of most people with the same problem. They simply cannot differentiate real dangers from potential ones and tend to internalize potential threats as something that is going to happen to them no matter what. Reasoning doesn't work here.

Dr. John

October 22 — Diary Entries

2:00 PM

The road outside my window is growing jerkily wider than narrower. I know this is just a hallucination, but it is interesting nonetheless. The falling leaves are turning into butterflies, orange in color. These hallucinations are actually pleasant one indeed. Axil knows that I am tripping, for he is at my side. I don't know why I am hallucinating. This is the way it has always been. At least I am not hearing those awful voices at this time.

8:00 PM

I spent the last few hours lying on my back. The pain is literally awful. On the 27th I will get my operation. The operation will be the beginning of the end of my physical pain. Too bad this can't be done with my mind.

October 22 — Commentary

These two entries are hallucinations, which Danny can recognize as such. He is very descriptive of these hallucinations. Not all hallucinations are terrifying.

Danny tells me that hallucinations are present every day of his life. This is the hallmark of his illness. Both stress and fear can be precipitating factors.

Most people with schizophrenia live with constant fear which soon leads to apathy. Anticipation and fear of his scheduled surgery has been hard for him to handle because of his already stressed mind.

Dr. John

October 23 — Diary Entries

1:00 AM

The television is on and the people on the TV are finishing my sentences. It's almost as if they can read my mind. I'm watching the news channel. The opinions (not the actual news) are all mine. My voices are telling me that I should turn off the TV because it's the devil. They say that he is trying to take control of my mind.

4:00 PM

My mom just went to bed after helping me get through a panic attack. I really hate panic attacks, especially psychotic ones that I get. The only way I could explain them is they are worse than dying. I often pray for death when I am going through them.

Axil just chased two does in the front yard. He stopped at the edge of the yard and sat down realizing he could not catch them.

4:00 PM

Since I did not sleep last night, I just woke up. I was dreaming about eating potato chips in a contest. The contest was in the desert and was held in order to be sure I got enough salt, so I wouldn't get dehydrated.

6:00 PM

I am feeling weird right now. I will try to explain. My whole body feels numb. I think very slow and burnt our right now. I sometimes think what it would be like to be normal. Hell, what is normality? What would it be like to not hear voices or not see visual hallucinations? I have been psychotic my whole life! All I have known is abnormality. I don't know what it would be like to have one thought at a time.

10:00 PM

What is normal? If someone is blind from birth, what is their sense of their surroundings? How do they perceive the world? Someone from the Congo in Africa is at home in their jungle. What would the New Yorker need to do to adapt to a Peruvian rain forest? The point that I am making is that what is normal to me might be an LSD trip to the average person. I seriously doubt that an average person could make it (without committing suicide) if they were suddenly immersed in my world. I wonder, if I lost all of my world and turned into an average person what would become of me? Would I commit suicide because of boredom or would I risk my life by skydiving and other stimulus seeking behaviors. I just wonder.

October 23 — Commentary

The entries of this day are really representative of the true deeper feelings of a person with schizophrenia. Beneath the veneer of the mentally ill person is the true person who wants questions answered.

Dr. John

October 25 — Diary Entries

2:30 PM

I couldn't write until now. For the past 24 hours I've been lying on the floor because of back pain. Pain, as I experience it, is the inability to move. Everything gets tight and pinches me. Right now, I'm doing better, but I'm still having stiff legs. This makes walking difficult. I'm still having olfactory hallucinations. I am smelling cinnamon and cherry scents. This is pleasurable for a while but becomes a pain in the ass after 24 hours. I might as well have a cherry-cinnamon piece of candy in my mouth.

4:00 PM

The sunlight in my window seems to draw me to it. I feel entranced with it. I know that if I stare at it I will blind myself. So I must go to another room. I feel like a bug attracted to a light at night.

6:00 PM

Axil ate at 5 PM, but is now asking for something to eat. He is also telling me that he wants to cuddle. Sometimes I wonder why I am the only one who can hear him. Granted, he's a dog, but he's telepathic. I hear him just as loud as anyone else.

8:00 PM

Why do I like nicotine? Personally, I don't know any schizophrenic who doesn't smoke or chew tobacco. As for me, I think that nicotine hits the cingulated gyrus, much the same way as cocaine. I have either smokes or chewed tobacco most of my life. I've tried cocaine and it felt like smoking a cigar. There you have it. Schizophrenics love tobacco.

October 25 — Commentary

By now Danny's personality is recognizable to the reader. You are beginning to understand how his mind works. You are probably asking yourself, it if were you, could you take the constant dream world that Danny calls wonderland?

Danny's motto of "never give up" has helped carry him through his illness. He has few pleasurable activities. Smoking is one of them. He is aware of the potential cancer causing effect. His reply is, "So what?" I can understand why.

Dr. John

November 11 — Diary Entries

1:00 PM

I haven't written in a while because I have been in too much pain due to a triple fusion in my lower back. Sitting upright has not been in my vocabulary for some time now (2 weeks). However, it's a fact that psychological pain is much more powerful than physical pain.

7:00 PM

My ears have been ringing all day long. It sounds like high-pitched white noise. Nevertheless it's almost unbearable. Axil tells me he wants to eat. Christ, he's eaten a whole bowl of dog chow already. Axil also has ringing ears, with the exception that his ears put out noises.

9:00 PM

I really hate it when a mass-murderer is referred to as being psychotic or just mentally schizophrenic. If you are not a neophyte or psychological scientist, then you will be able to explain to the fucking idiots on the news channels that it is those people, who aren't suffering mental illness but those with religion problems.

11:00 PM

My back feels like it's behind me by 4 inches. That's because I feel like I'm behind myself. I'm not interacting with my environment. I am watching everything unfold as though it was yesterday. I'm experiencing déjà on steroids. It doesn't matter what happens, who says what, or what is going to happen. It has already happened somehow.

November 11 — Commentary

In this entry Danny explains his reason for his absence. After undergoing major spinal fusion surgery he still feels that mental pain is worse than physical pain. Many other people with schizophrenia would agree with him. Schizophrenia doesn't cause physical pain, but it still causes pain.

Dr. John

November 12 — Diary Entries

12:00 PM

The day is bright and sunny. However the house that was talking to me earlier this morning is now a glowing blue. That's a weird color for a green house to become. It must be haunted. I should know, because houses don't' normally talk with their windows closed.

4:30 PM

Axil just woke me up with his muzzle, saying I need to sleep tonight. He was right. My sleep schedule has been erratic in nature lately. I don't sleep at all for what seems like days, Then I sleep for 28 hours straight. I think everyone is a little crazy in one aspect or another. Take for instance, baseball players. They're so full of obsessive-compulsive, superstitious behavior that they become nervous wrecks when at bat.

6:00 PM

Today has gone by extremely quickly. I hope that I can go see my brother Joe's soccer game tonight at 10:00 PM. I feel trapped in this house. I want to get out. Sure I'm hallucinating and in a lot of pain, but I need a change of scenery.

November 12 — Commentary

This day has started as usual for Danny, full of hallucination and delusion. Getting the feel of the thoughts of a person with schizophrenia is exactly what this diary is intended to do. It is for those of us who are thankful to call ourselves "normal".

Dr. John

November 13 — Diary Entries

4:30 PM

I just awakened from bed. Like I said earlier, my sleep schedule is off. This could be due to bipolar shifting. I don't know. What I do know is that I probably could sleep until tomorrow or longer. I am going to try to stay awake with coffee and cigarettes. Hell, even my father just woke up.

6:00 PM

I finally am no longer over-stimulated, However the refrigerator is still breathing in and out. In addition the cabinets are asthmatically trying to breathe. I, for one, am having no trouble whatsoever with breathing.

10:00 PM

I can hear my heartbeat outside of my ears. My mind is now a thousand synapses encircling my eyes. What the hell?, I'm not having a very good day. This truly sucks to suffer like this. And to think, people actually take mind expanding drugs to be like this? They are the ones who have lost their marbles.

November 13 — Commentary

As you have read this diary you undoubtedly asked yourself, "What is normal?" The best gift you can give to a troubled person is your time being a concerned listener.

Dr. John

November 14 — Diary Entries

12:00 PM

Today is a lot less stimulating than yesterday. I feel a bit crispy. I ended up not sleeping last night. I got manic last night. I thought I could just sleep. I still wonder why people take drugs to get like me. I don't like drugs. They give me panic attacks. Cigarettes make be feel euphoric. That's as close to drugs as I will ever get. Hell. I take drugs like Haldol to stop hallucinating. They really just limit my hallucinating to a livable point. I really think that there will never be a drug that will stop my hallucinating. Doctors keep saying that it is only a matter of time. I'm not holding my breath.

3:00 PM

Every schizophrenic should have a pet. For me, Axil is a lifesaver. He is the first to know when I have not taken my medications. One time, I was in bed having a panic attack. Apparently, I had forgotten my last scheduled Klonopin. I had forgotten to take it. Axil used his muzzle to push me out of bed and walked over and got my med box and took it to me. I understood and took my missed dose.

November 14 — Commentary

These entries reflect the logical thinking of Danny, which without the stabilization of his prescribed medication would probably not be possible. The 12:00 entry reflects some of my casual comments to Danny about illicit drug use. I am encouraged by the progress of psychiatric medicine over the last twenty plus years. We must continue the research with new pharmacologic drugs and continue with the education of the general public worldwide in order to continue to make progress in psychiatric medicine.

In my lifetime we have done away with asylums. Society does not like to talk about our failures, only our successes. I guess this is our human nature. We don't like to talk about holocaust or genocide because we are ashamed of our failures. Some people want to keep this out of the history books. Wrong!

We cannot hide our mistakes. We must admit them. Accept them; live with the truth. It is now time to help those with mental illness, not punish them for a condition beyond their control.

Dr. John

November 15 — Diary Entries

12:00 PM

Today may prove to be an extraordinary day. I am hallucinating, but not to the point of immobility. It's warm outside (60). And only partly cloudy, Axil says he's in a good mood. My mood is on the high side. I am only slightly manic.

4:00 PM

I've been cuddling Axil for the last 3 hours. I say blue butterflies flying around with the naked fairies for quite some time. They all appeared to be in synchrony with each other. I had to constantly wipe off pixie dust, because I did not want to fly away with those fairies. Axil was a good anchor, for he was under a blanket. Axil is a large dog, weighing about 140 pounds.

November 16 — Diary Entries

1:00 PM

My lack of bathing caught my dad's attention. He told me that I needed to shower and shave. I complied. All too often, I tried to forget about my appearance. When I'm actively being tortured mentally, I tend to forget about the outside world in which we live.

5:00 PM

I'm definitely on the depressed side of the continuum. I've been sleeping for some time now. Axil woke me up to tell me it was dinner time. I just laid down, or I thought I did. I'm probably going back to sleep after dinner. Being depressed is like going to another planet where the gravity is much greater, and it's an effort to stay awake.

November 16 — Commentary

Just when you think that things are finally normal with Danny's thought process, you definitely can see that the hallucinations are there all along. Schizophrenia is a frustrating illness that doesn't get better.

Delusions can be difficult to spot when talking with the person having the delusion because they appear so matter of fact and so earnestly believed by the person with the delusion that they become almost impossible to isolate.

Do not argue with the person experiencing the delusion by saying. "That's impossible," but rather be pleasant and ask him or her to tell you more about it. Remember to be a good listener.

Dr. John

November 17 — Diary Entries

12:00 PM

I am currently very down and out. My sleep was excellent, but I woke up soaked with sweat. I changed shirts and am now writing. It's very difficult to stay awake. My mind is focused on morbid thoughts. Today I plan on spending as much time as I can on talking to and holding Axil. Hopefully my mom will come home from church soon, so I can physically get out. Even grocery shopping would help ease my depressed mood.

3:00 PM

I called my psychiatrist earlier and am awaiting his return call. This depression is truly of bipolar origin. I was feeling terrific for a while, and then the floor fell our beneath me. How have I been waiting?, sleeping of course!

5:00 PM

My psychiatrist still hasn't called yet. I'm feeling worse now. I'm hearing voices argue as to whether or not I should kill myself. Luckily the argument that I should persevere is winning out. I'm just frustrated. I wish these damned voices would just stop. I also wish my doctor would call now.

November 17 — Commentary

Danny's life has become very dependent on the return phone calls and advice of his doctors. He is very compliant in that he does exactly what he is told. He takes his medicine exactly as instructed and on time. His mother and I have instructed him how to divide up his daily doses by using compartmentalized pill containers. Developing this little habit adds to control and compliance.

Dr. John

November 21 — Diary Entries

The last three days I spent time with three problems. First, I was having commanding hallucinations. The voices were telling me to kill myself. This took me to the edge. I was very confused. Second I was severely depressed, I was numb to the outside world. Third I was dealing with severe (post-op) back pain. For the second one I called my psychiatrist and had my Effexor increased by 75 mgm. For the third problem, extreme pain. I just dealt with it, and I still am.

3:00 PM

I've been laying down and talking with Axil. My pain level is quite high, and my visions have been forthcoming.

7:00 PM

Life is a whirlwind and if you let it pass you by, it's your fault. When in pain, deal with it. When hallucinating like I am right now, let it flow. I'm in pain and hearing voices congratulating me for making it through another day. That's odd; I rarely get a pat on the back for suffering.

November 21 — Commentary

The same two problems are again apparent: the delusion of talking to Axil and hallucinations. Danny recognizes the hallucinations as such but the talking to Axil continues to be viewed as normal.

Danny has some very special abilities at playing chess. Interpreting what he reads or sees on T.V., computer skills, or doing complex math. He is knowledgeable and especially skilled in target shooting with an air rifle, which is his hobby. He is very knowledgeable and has practically memorized the Bible. According to his psychologist he has an extremely high IQ and a photographic memory.

Dr. John

November 22 — Diary Entries

12:00 PM

I was up all night and hearing voices. The pain in my back was unbearable. I could not get comfortable no matter what position I was in. The voices were whispers telling me to kill myself. When an hour had passed, I could take no more. I woke up my mom and asked her to sit with me. We talked all night.

5:00 PM

I've laid in bed pretty much all day not sleeping. I tried to watch TV, but it was broadcasting all of my thoughts. This was quite unnerving. I called Axil into my room and he cuddles and slept by my side. What a wonderful dog he is.
7:00 PM Axil tells me that I'll sleep tonight. I highly doubt it, for I am hallucinating and in a lot of pain. Axil holds to the "roller-coaster" theory, while I hold to the "shit happens" theory. Axil is a little more talkative today. I wonder why.

9:00 PM

I do not know what is more troubling, the intense back pain or the negative hallucinations. Right now, I just want to be knocked out and escape this torment. I would also like to wake up and be in a better mood.

November 22 — Commentary

We have had to be good listeners as family supporters of Danny. Danny always turns to his support base, his family, when he can't handle the stress of his life with schizophrenia. My wife and I realize that we will from time to time need to sit up with Danny and be good listeners. How do we do it? Well, it is all about putting someone else ahead of yourself. By doing this we have found a new, deeper love and a stronger family relationship.

A similar relationship is experienced by families caring for a special needs family member. The care is needed so it is unselfishly given. Some people in the population of the world will not be able to be caregivers because they are too self-centered.

Dr. John

FINAL WORDS by Daniel

I have had schizophrenia since early childhood, and acquired insight when I was twelve years old. This took place gradually over time through a variety of factors and circumstances. The following list of suggestions was instrumental in my developing discernment about having schizophrenia, and in my successfully helping other individuals with the disorder to progress toward insight.

• Learn to recognize warning signs for onset or crisis. Schizophrenia does not usually start with an acute psychotic crisis. It often starts with early warning signs that gradually build in intensity, such as insomnia, social withdrawal, deterioration of personal hygiene, paranoia, hostility, confusing speech and hallucinations. The child may lose desire to see friends or interact socially, become confused in his speech during a daily routine, have outbursts of hostility or anger, describe hearing or seeing things that don't exist, or stare seemingly at nothing for an unusually long time. If the child is demonstrating any of these, remain calm, do not express irritation or alarm, and make an appointment to see a mental health professional.

• Consult with a pediatric psychiatrist, who will recommend seeing a therapist and prescribe anti-psychotic medication. Therapy can help the child talk about difficult emotions, communicate his concerns about symptoms and learn coping skills to deal with symptoms effectively. Anti-psychotic medications may not always eliminate hallucinations entirely, but they do cause them to fade or become less intense, which helps a child with psychotic symptoms to focus more on what is real. Anti-psychotics help create a type of balance consisting of more reality vs. less psychosis, helping to generate clear thinking. Anti-anxiety medications, often prescribed along with anti-psychotics, help manage reactions and calm anxiety about the hallucinations and delusions.

• Engage frequently in active listening to the child. Spend time asking her to tell you about what she thinks, feels, sees, hears, tastes and smells. Allow her to unload and express her feelings and experiences without fear of judgment or criticism. Talking helps dispel the intensity and power of hallucinations and delusions, and will help reduce fear and anxiety. Hallucinations and delusions are as real to the affected child as they are unreal to those who do not have symptoms. When she describes a hallucination or delusion, say, "That must be very frightening. (or funny, stressful, etc). I understand you're frightened (or laughing or upset), and I believe you hear it (or see it), but I don't hear that voice (or see that object). Can you tell me about it? Do you think it's real? Can you tell me the difference between a real thing and a hallucination or delusion? Can you try to ignore it? Would it be helpful for you if we play a game together?" Be alert to negative or harmful patterns or themes the child may tell you about or demonstrate. Ask her, "Is there a voice telling you to do something?" "Do you think what it's telling you to do is good or bad? Can you think of something to do or say that's a better choice?" Ask him, "Do you feel like hurting yourself or others?" If the child is communicating anything that sounds potentially harmful, medical intervention should be sought.

- Encourage the child to develop thought stopping strategies, which will help him to feel in control. Suggest he try to control his thoughts by humming, singing, listening to or playing music, reading, talking to someone, exercising, taking a walk, holding up her hand as if pushing it away, ignoring the voice or object. Suggest he try to focus on a person, animal or thing that is a known constant. If possible, adopt a pet. Playing with and caring for a pet can bring out his nurturing instinct and help him feel needed. A pet can be a source of security and comfort, and can help him progress toward insight by focusing his attention on real things.

- Practice acceptance. Although there is no cure for schizophrenia, symptoms can be managed through coping strategies and medication. Schizophrenia can be defined as a thought disorder, and assisting a child to distinguish real thoughts from psychotic thoughts is a critical part of guiding her toward recovery. The process of achieving insight, or learning to "think about one's thinking" requires an immense commitment of time, effort and patience from the child and his or her caretaker. Empowering the child with affirmative statements, such as, "There is something special about your brain that makes you hear, see and think things that other people don't. These things are called hallucinations and delusions. Nothing is "wrong" with your brain, it just works differently than other people, just as people have different eye colors, personalities or abilities," can help normalize the disorder, reduce anxiety and foster a sense of control.

• Cultivate an atmosphere of optimism, joy and affection. Build confidence and self-reliance through affirmations that she is special, unique, and talented. Embrace joy daily by seeking out fun and pleasurable activities to do with her. Practice gratefulness by asking her to mention something to be thankful about every day.

www.ingramcontent.com/pod-product-compliance
Lightning Source LLC
Chambersburg PA
CBHW050540280326
41933CB00011B/1658